Table of Contents

About the Writers

Julia Olson got her start teaching piano in Utah, where she also taught preschool at a private school that emphasized learning through music. Since then, she has taught private piano lessons as well as early childhood music and group piano classes in California and Illinois. She is a member of the National Music Teachers Association and the Early Childhood Music and Movement Association. In addition to maintaining a piano studio with children of all ages, Julia directs children's choirs in her community.

Kevin Olson is an active pianist, composer, and member of the piano faculty at Utah State University, where he teaches piano literature, pedagogy, and accompanying courses. In addition to his collegiate teaching responsibilities, Kevin directs the Utah State Youth Conservatory, which provides weekly group and private piano instruction to more than 200 pre-college, community students. Before teaching at Utah State, he was on the faculty at Elmhurst College near Chicago and Humboldt State University in northern California.

He also writes and edits music for The FJH Music Company, which he joined as a writer in 1994. Many of the needs of his own piano students have inspired a diverse collection of books and solos he has published of original music and instructional material. Kevin received his Bachelor's and Master's degrees in Music Composition & Theory from Brigham Young University, and holds a Doctorate of Education from National-Louis University.

Kevin and Julia live in Logan, Utah with their four children: Skyler, Casey, Aubery, and Wesley.

FJH2150

A few things to remember about music...

Beat and Tempo

Music makes you want to tap your feet because it has a beat, like a beating drum. Listen to the beat in all the music you hear. See if you can clap or tap to the beat. The beat in music can be fast, slow, or in the middle. This is called *tempo*. A metronome can help you set a tempo for your music. You might want to purchase a metronome for practice at home.

Tempo Settings

There are many different words to describe tempo settings in music. Some of the more common tempo settings are *largo, andante,* and *allegro.* Set your metronome to these tempo settings and clap to the beat.

Largo	**Andante**	**Allegro**
40–60	76–108	120–168

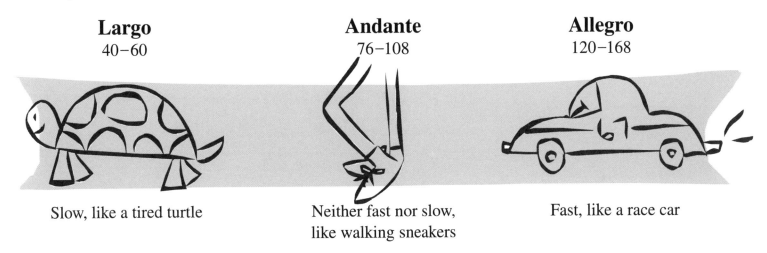

| Slow, like a tired turtle | Neither fast nor slow, like walking sneakers | Fast, like a race car |

Dynamic Markings

Music can be soft, loud, or in the middle. There are words to describe how soft or loud you can play. These words are called *dynamics.* Play some keys on the piano to make them sound soft, loud, or in the middle.

p is for *piano*   *m* is for *mezzo*   *f* is for *forte*

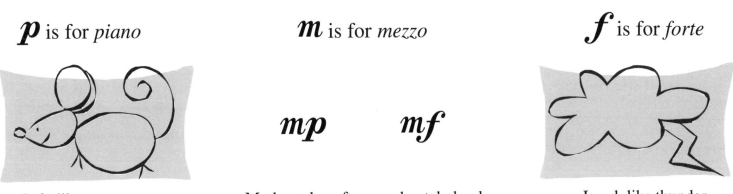

mp   *mf*

| Soft, like a mouse | Moderately soft or moderately loud (in the middle) | Loud, like thunder |

A few things to remember about counting...

Notes and Note Values

In music, there are many different types of notes. Some notes are held for a short amount of time and others are held longer. To play music, you will need to know how many beats each note is worth.

Quarter Note	Half Note	Dotted Half Note	Whole Note
1 Beat	2 Beats	3 Beats	4 Beats
Clap and say 1	Clap and HOLD say 1 2	Clap and HOLD say 1 2 3	Clap and HOLD say 1 2 3 4

Rests and Rest Values

Sometimes in music, we take a short break before we play again. This is called a *rest*.
There are different types of rests and rest values as well.

Quarter Rest	Half Rest	Whole Rest
1 Beat of Silence	2 Beats of Silence	3 or 4
say 1	say 1 2	Beats of Silence say 1 2 3 or 1 2 3 4

FJH2156

Bar Lines and Measures

To keep music notes and rests organized, there are lines called *bar lines*. The beats between the bar lines make up *measures*. At the end of a song, you will see a *double bar line*. The bar lines and measures help us count our music. You will count the beats in each measure and start over on beat 1 each time you come to a bar line or a new measure.

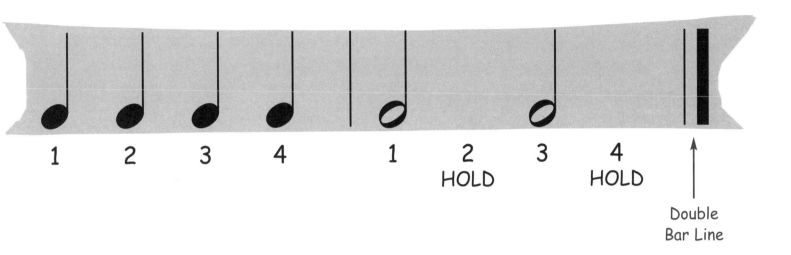

Time Signature

At the beginning of your music you will find a *time signature*. The time signature has a top number and a bottom number. The top number tells you how many beats are in each measure and the bottom number tells you the type of note that gets the beat. (For now, it will usually be the quarter note.)

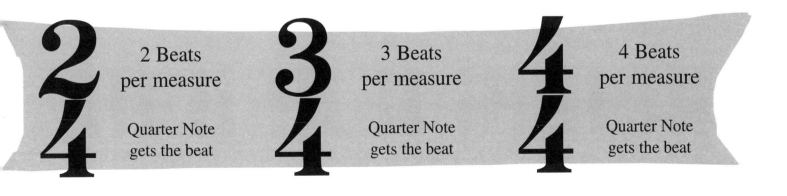

A few things to remember about playing the piano...

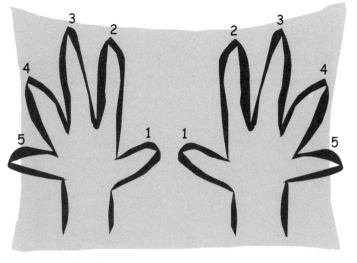

Left Hand
(L.H.)

Right Hand
(R.H.)

Finger Numbers

Each of your fingers has a number assigned to it for playing the piano.

Thumb is finger number 1.
Pointer finger is finger number 2.
Tall finger is finger number 3.
Ring finger is finger number 4.
Pinky is finger number 5.

Wiggle each of your fingers and mix it up for review.

The Piano Keyboard

The piano keyboard is made up of many keys, with high notes to the right and low notes to the left. There are both white keys and black keys. The black keys are in groups of 2 and 3.

Play and count all the 2-black-key groups on your piano.

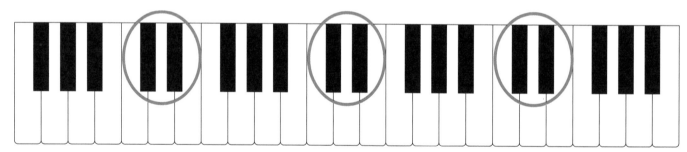

Play and count all the 3-black-key groups on your piano.

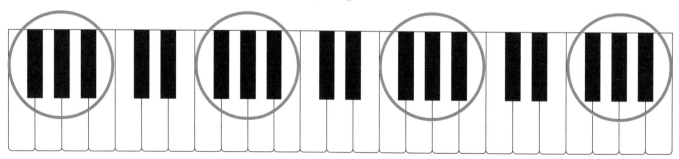

FJH2150

The Musical Alphabet

The musical alphabet is different than the regular alphabet.
The musical alphabet goes up to G but then starts all over at A again, like this:

A B C D E F G A B C D E F G A B C etc.

The White Keys

The musical alphabet is repeated over and over on the white keys. Play all the white keys starting with the first one on the left, which is A. Sing the musical alphabet as you play.

Continue ⟶

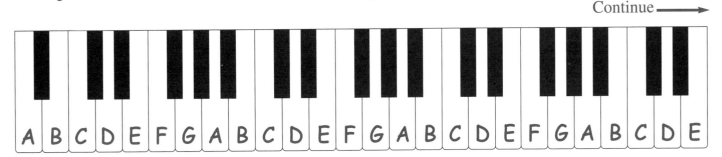

Because there are *so* many white keys, it helps to look at the 2-black-key groups to learn them. Below each 2-black-key group you will always find CDE, and below each 3-black-key group you will always find FGAB.

Octaves

Every 8 notes, a key is repeated. These are called *octaves*. For example, look at all of the C's on the keyboard below. These C's are different octaves but they are all C's. The C's to the left are the lower C's and the C's to the right are the higher C's.

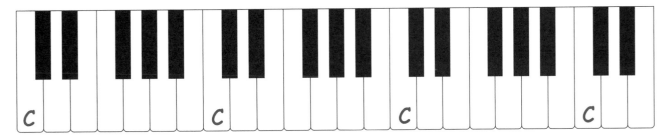

A few things to remember about note reading...

The Grand Staff

Music notes are written on a group of lines and spaces called a *staff*. A staff has 5 lines and 4 spaces. Piano music is written on two staves (staffs) grouped together called the *grand staff*. The top staff is called the treble staff and the bottom staff is called the bass staff.

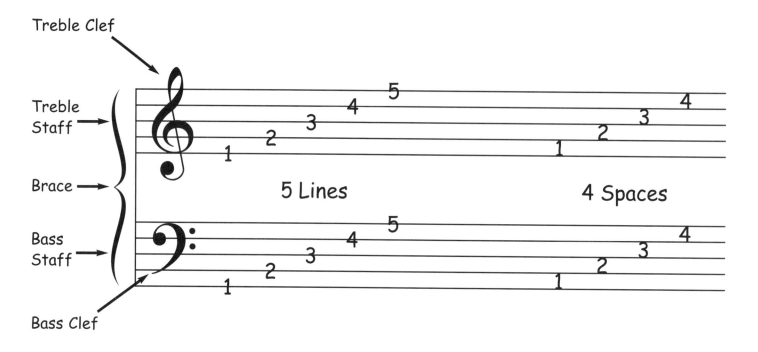

The Musical Alphabet on the Staff

Right hand usually plays all the notes that are written on the treble staff.
Left hand usually plays all the notes that are written on the bass staff.

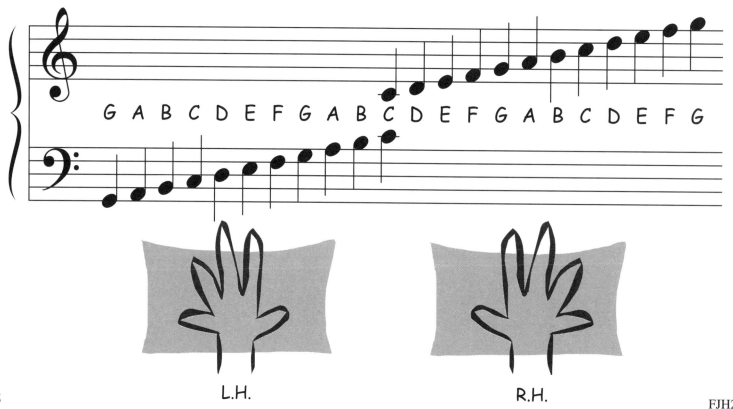

FJH2150

Low G Hand Position for the Left Hand*

The first group of notes in this book are with the right hand in C Position and the left hand in Low G Position. To play with the left hand in Low G Position, place the left-hand thumb on the D below Middle C. Place the rest of your fingers as indicated in the guide below.

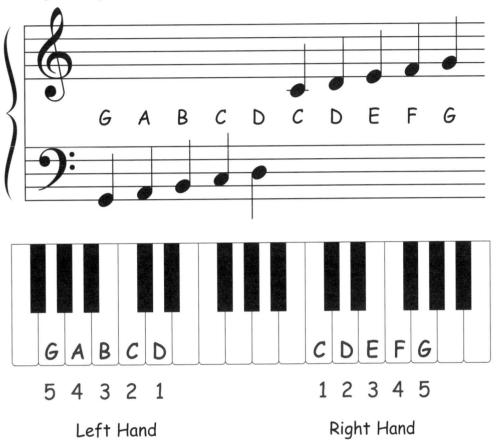

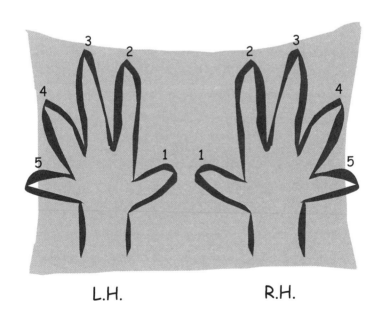

L.H.   R.H.

*Remember hand positions are only "guides" that help you feel comfortable learning new notes. Once you are comfortable, explore your pieces further by starting on a different finger.

G A B C D on the Keyboard

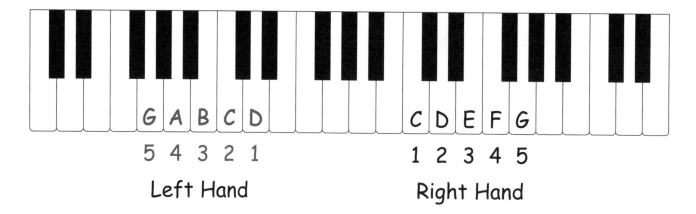

Left Hand   Right Hand

Remember that hand positions are just guides. When you are comfortable with the pieces in this unit, explore using different fingers.

G A B C D on the Bass Staff

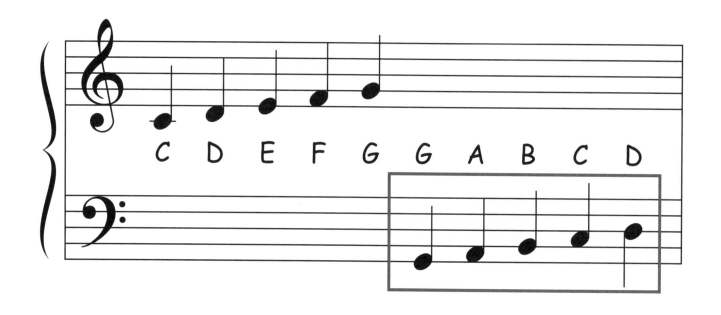

Play the example below, keeping your eyes on the music.

Note Guide

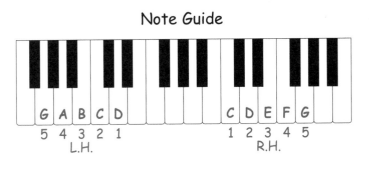

Cactus

Andante

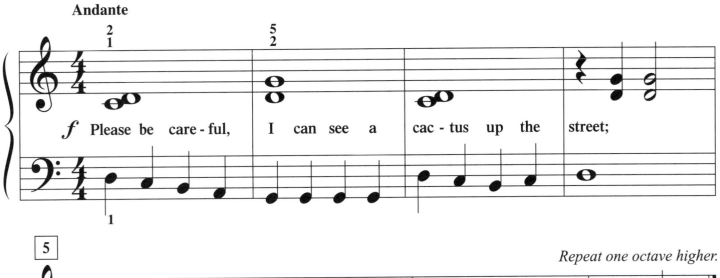

f Please be care - ful, I can see a cac - tus up the street;

Repeat one octave higher.

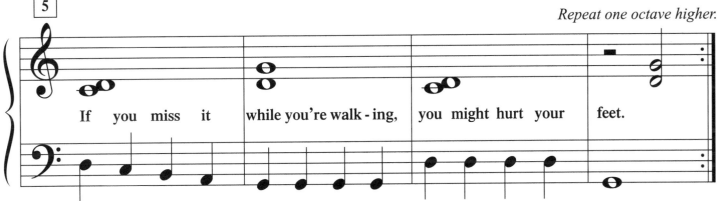

If you miss it while you're walk - ing, you might hurt your feet.

Teacher Duet: Student plays one octave higher.

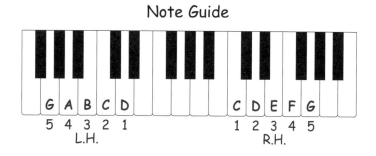

Note Guide

Missing Shoe

Andante

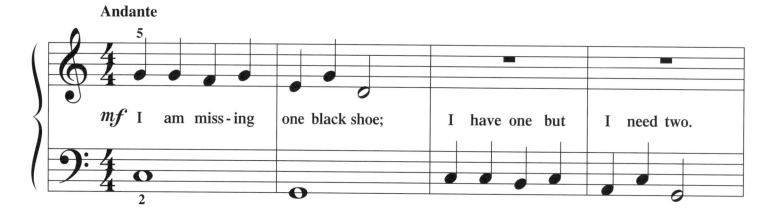

mf I am miss-ing one black shoe; I have one but I need two.

Repeat one octave higher.

If my shoe is real-ly lost, I will go to school in socks.

Teacher Duet: Student plays one octave higher.

FJH2150

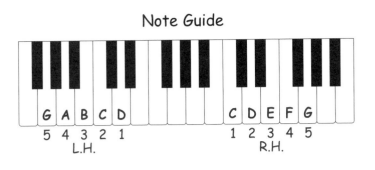

Note Guide

Silly Old Troll

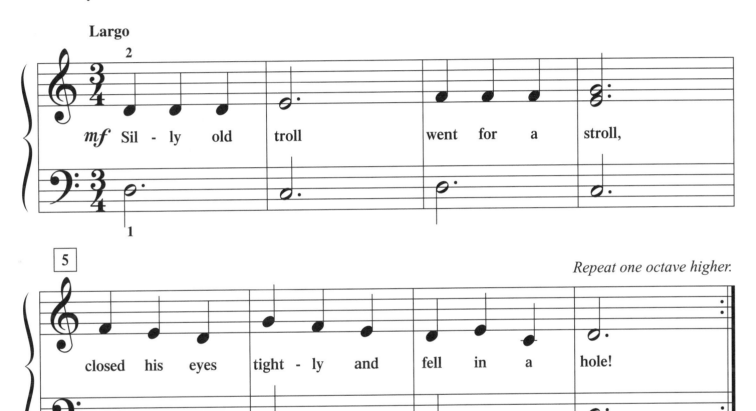

Largo

mf Sil - ly old troll went for a stroll,

5 closed his eyes tight - ly and fell in a hole!

Repeat one octave higher.

After you are comfortable with this piece, try playing with **L.H.** finger **2** on **D.**

Teacher Duet: Student plays one octave higher.

Note Guide

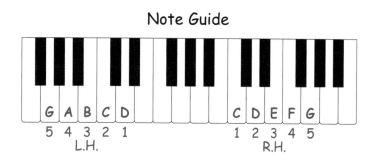

Woodpecker

Andante

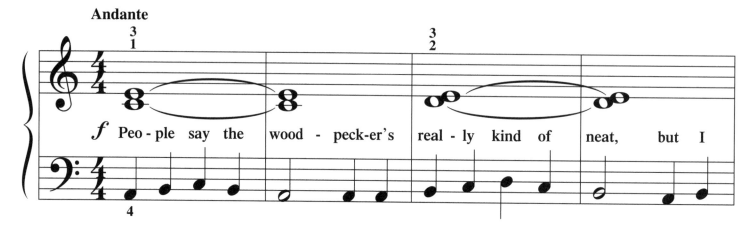

f Peo - ple say the wood - peck-er's real - ly kind of neat, but I

Repeat one octave higher.

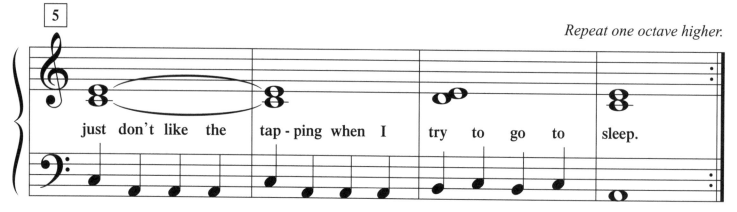

just don't like the tap - ping when I try to go to sleep.

After you are comfortable with this piece, try playing with **L.H.** finger **5** on **A.**

Teacher Duet: Student plays one octave higher.

14

FJH2150

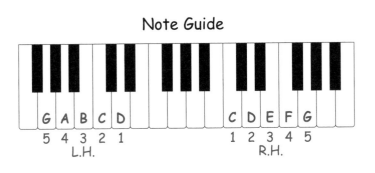

Note Guide

Purple Car

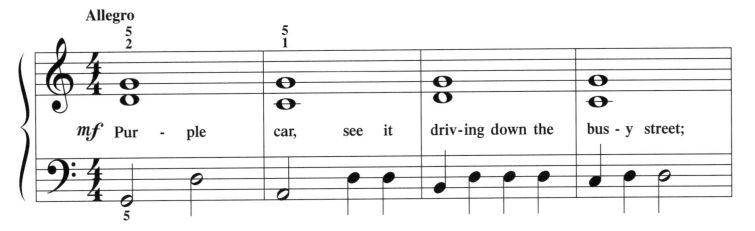

Allegro

mf Pur - ple car, see it driv-ing down the bus - y street;

Out of all the cars I've seen, the pur - ple ones just can't be beat!

Repeat one octave higher.

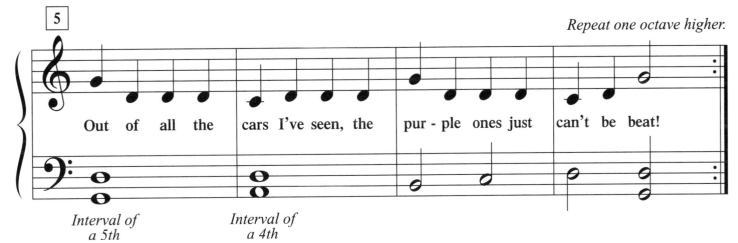

Interval of a 5th   *Interval of a 4th*

Teacher Duet: Student plays one octave higher.

R.H.

L.H. *mp*

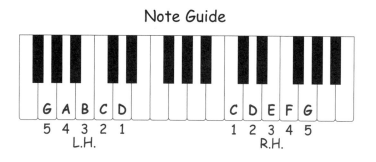

Note Guide

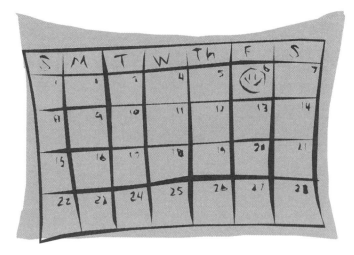

The Friday Song

Andante

f Fri - day, Fri - day, it's

Repeat one octave higher.

fi - nal - ly, fi - nal - ly Fri - day!

Teacher Duet: Student plays one octave higher.

16 FJH2150

G Hand Position for Both Hands*

The next group of notes in this book are with both hands in G Position. To play with the right hand in G Position, place the right-hand thumb on the G above Middle C. Place the rest of your fingers as indicated in the guide below.

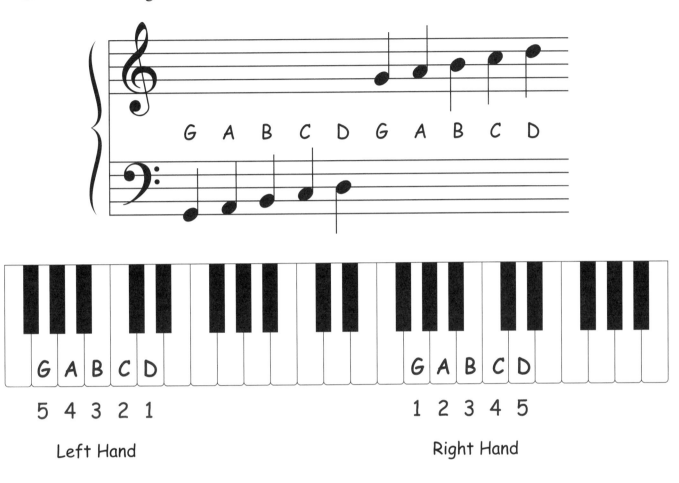

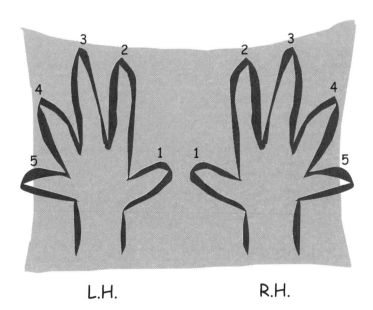

L.H.   R.H.

*Remember that hand positions are only "guides" that help you feel comfortable learning new notes. Once you are comfortable, remember to explore your pieces further by starting on a different finger.

Unit 2

G A B on the Keyboard

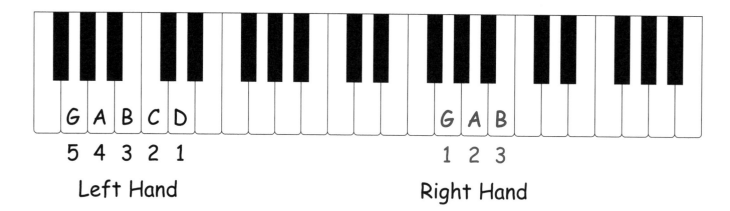

G A B C D
5 4 3 2 1
Left Hand

G A B
1 2 3
Right Hand

Remember that hand positions are just guides. When you are comfortable with the pieces in this unit, explore some of them using different fingers.

G A B on the Treble Staff

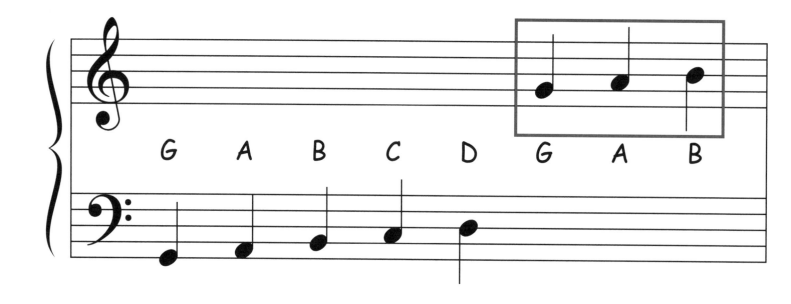

G   A   B   C   D   G   A   B

Play the example below, keeping your eyes on the music.

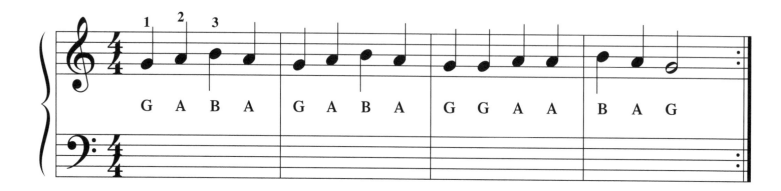

G A B A   G A B A   G G A A   B A G

FJH2150

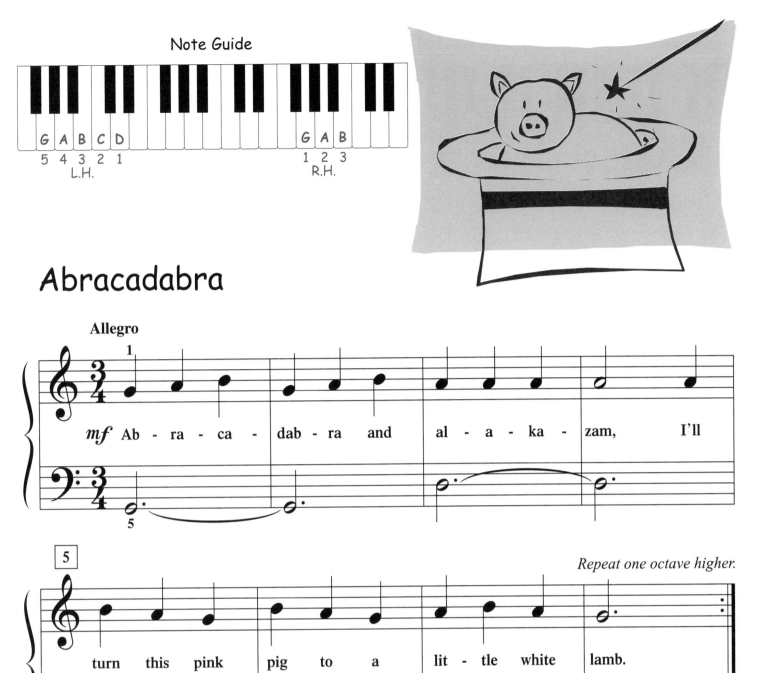

Abracadabra

Allegro

mf Ab - ra - ca - dab - ra and al - a - ka - zam, I'll

Repeat one octave higher.

turn this pink pig to a lit - tle white lamb.

After you are comfortable with this piece, try playing with **R.H.** finger **2** on **G.**

Teacher Duet: Student plays one octave higher.

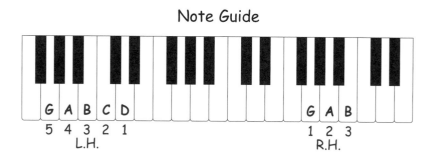

Note Guide

Hats

Andante

f I have two hats, may - be three or four;

Interval of a 3rd   *Interval of a 2nd*

Repeat one octave higher.

Five hats, six hats, may - be e - ven more.

After you are comfortable with this piece, try playing with **R.H.** finger **2** on **G.**

Teacher Duet: Student plays one octave higher.

mf

FJH2150

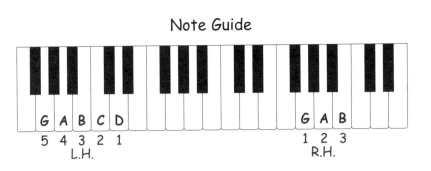

Note Guide

I Just Love to Vacuum

Andante

mf I just love to vac-uum. I think it's real-ly great to

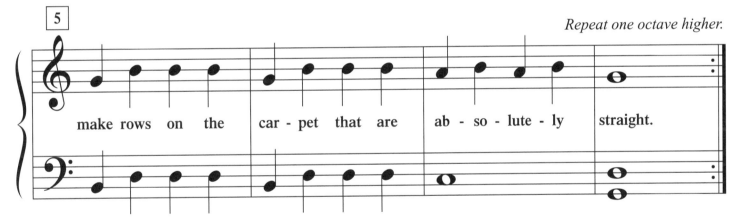

Repeat one octave higher.

make rows on the car-pet that are ab-so-lute-ly straight.

After you are comfortable with this piece, try playing with **R.H.** finger **3** on **G.**

Teacher Duet: Student plays one octave higher.

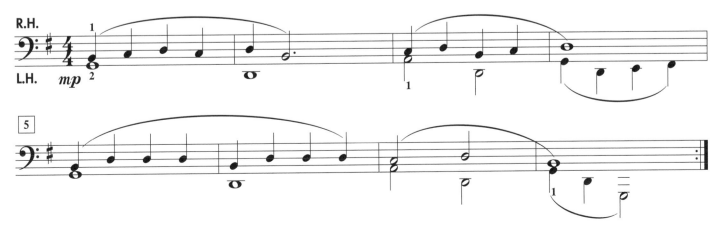

Note Guide

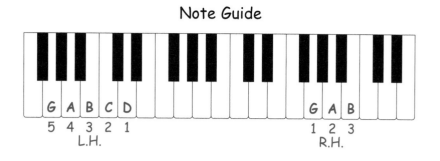

Too Many People

Allegro

f Too man - y peo - ple are in this crowd; I

Interval of a 2nd

Interval of a 3rd

5

Repeat one octave higher.

think they are cra - zy and way too loud.

After you are comfortable with this piece, try playing with **R.H.** fingers **2** and **3** on **G** and **A**.

Teacher Duet: Student plays one octave higher.

R.H.

L.H. mf

5

FJH2150

Note Guide

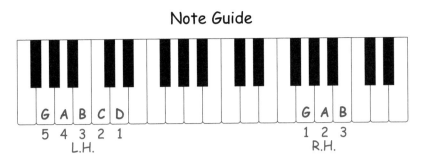

Sledding

Andante

mf Once I went sled - ding on my grand - pa's farm; I

fell down the hill and then I hurt my arm.

Repeat one octave higher.

After you are comfortable with this piece, try playing with **R.H.** fingers **2** and **4** on **G** and **B.**

Teacher Duet: Student plays one octave higher.

R.H.

L.H. *mp* *with pedal*

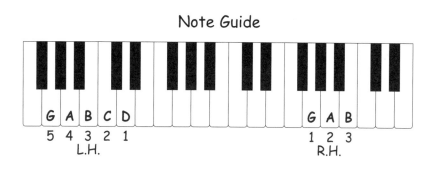

Rocket Ship

Allegro

mf If I had a rock-et ship, I'd let you come a - long, and

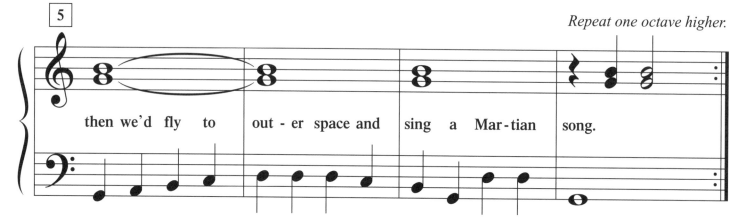

Repeat one octave higher.

then we'd fly to out-er space and sing a Mar-tian song.

After you are comfortable with this piece, try playing with **R.H.** fingers **2** and **4** on **G** and **B.**

Teacher Duet: Student plays one octave higher.

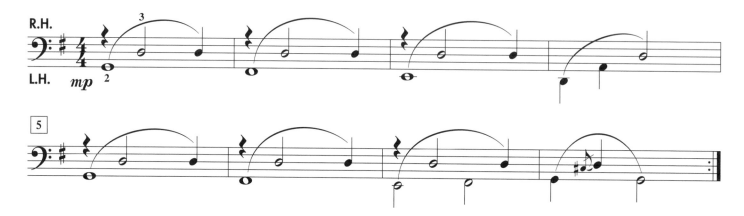

R.H.

L.H. *mp*

24

FJH2150

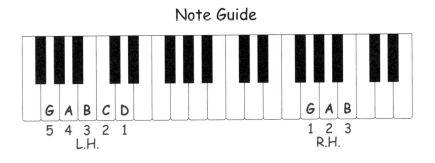

Note Guide

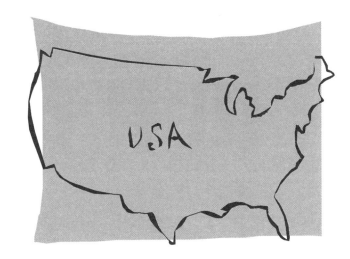

Fifty States

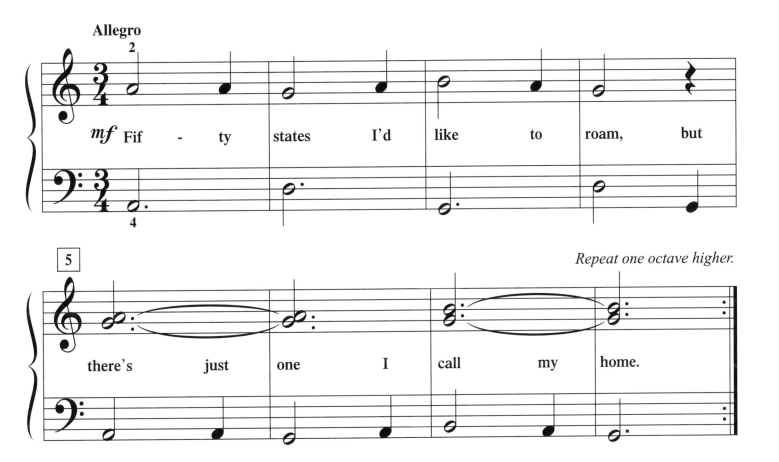

Allegro

mf Fif - ty states I'd like to roam, but

Repeat one octave higher.

there's just one I call my home.

After you are comfortable with this piece, try playing with **R.H.** finger **4** on **A.**

Teacher Duet: Student plays one octave higher.

Unit 3   C and D on the Keyboard

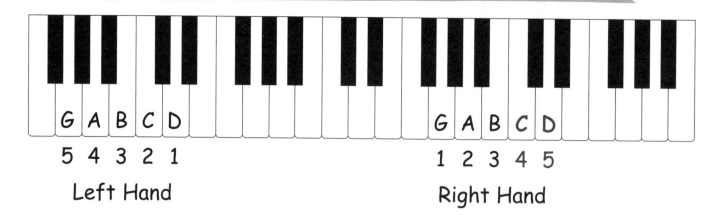

Remember that hand positions are just guides. When you are comfortable
with the pieces in this unit, explore using different fingers.

C and D on the Treble Staff

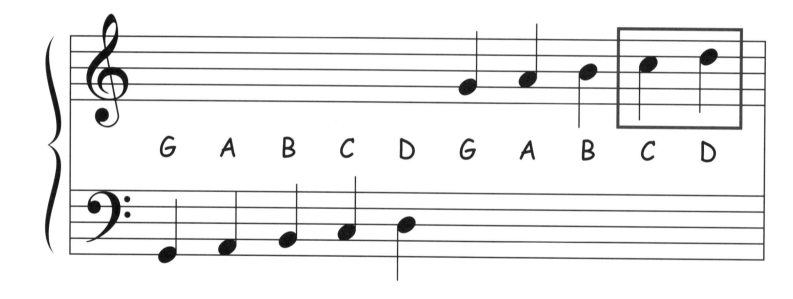

Play the example below, keeping your eyes on the music.

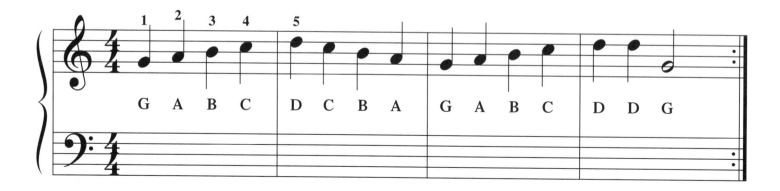

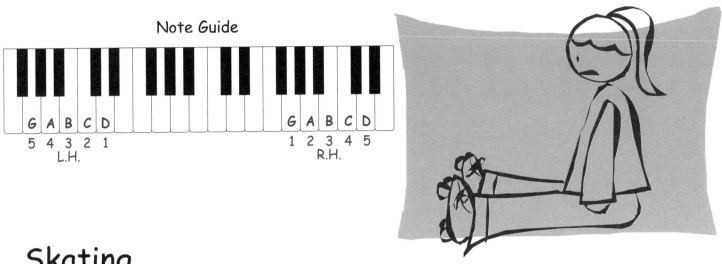

Note Guide

Skating

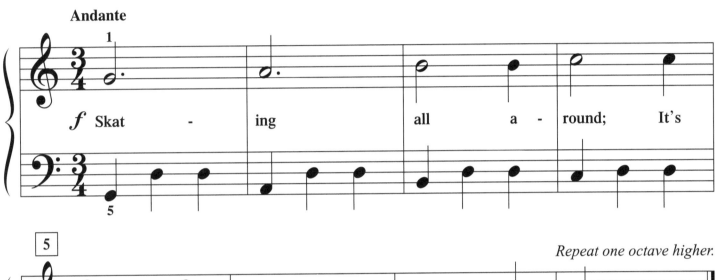

Andante

f Skat - ing all a - round; It's

Repeat one octave higher.

fun un - less I fall on the ground.

After you are comfortable with this piece, try playing it in **C Position.**

Teacher Duet: Student plays one octave higher.

FJH2150

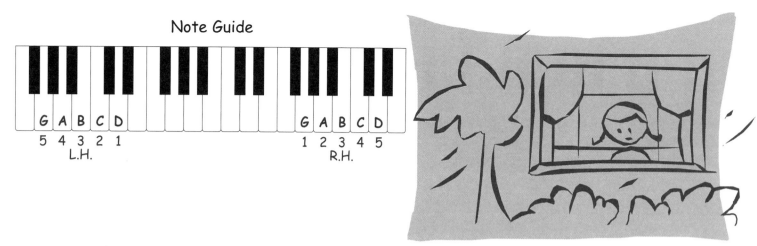

Note Guide

Windy Day

Andante

mf I don't want to play, on this wind - y day.

5

Repeat one octave higher.

I'm a - fraid that if I did then I would blow a - way.

After you are comfortable with this piece, try playing it in **C Position.**

Teacher Duet: Student plays one octave higher.

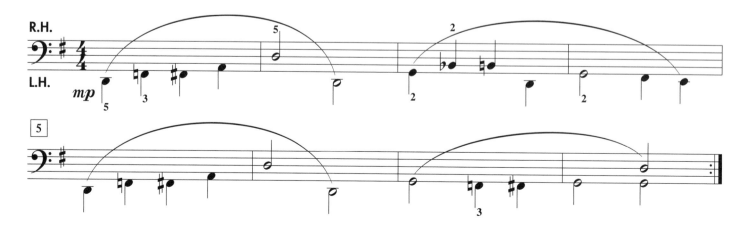

R.H.

L.H. *mp*

5

FJH2150

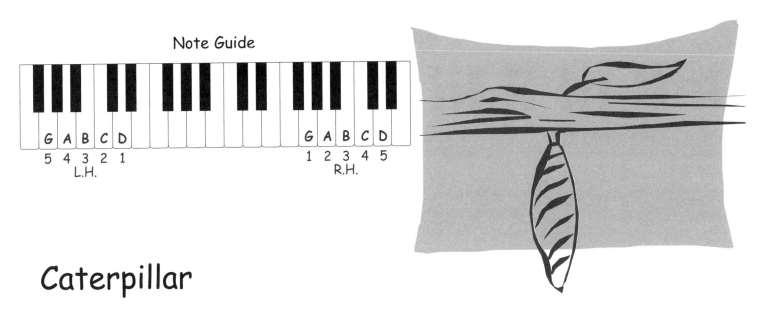

Note Guide

Caterpillar

Andante

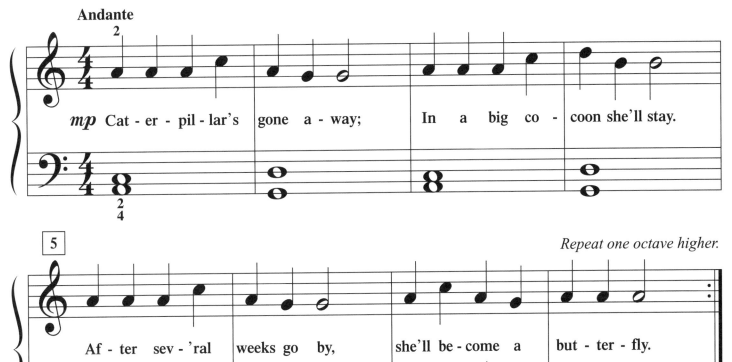

mp Cat - er - pil - lar's gone a - way; In a big co - coon she'll stay.

5

Repeat one octave higher.

Af - ter sev - 'ral weeks go by, she'll be - come a but - ter - fly.

After you are comfortable with this piece, try playing it in **C Position.**

Teacher Duet: Student plays one octave higher.

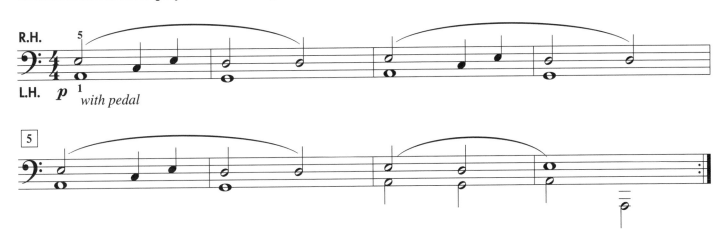

R.H. 5

L.H. *p* 1 *with pedal*

5

Note Guide

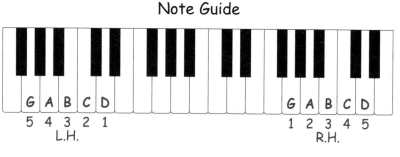

Apples for Lunch

Allegro

f I'm eat - ing ap - ples for lunch 'cause

Repeat one octave higher.

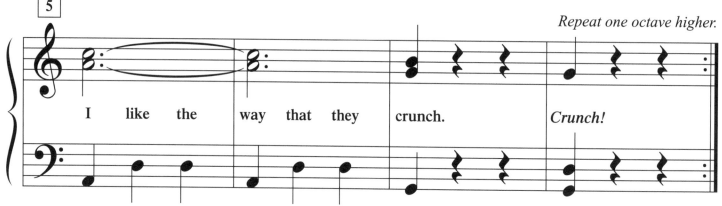

I like the way that they crunch. *Crunch!*

After you are comfortable with this piece, try playing it in **C Position.**

Teacher Duet: Student plays one octave higher.

FJH2150

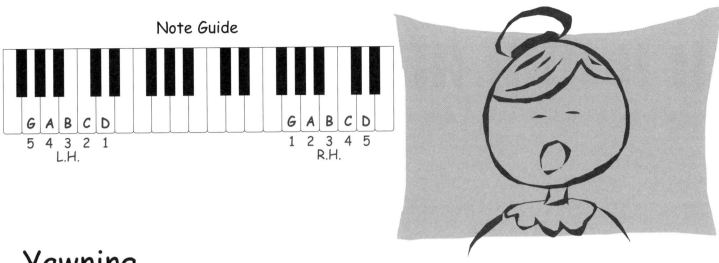

Note Guide

Yawning

Andante

Interval of a 4th

mp When you yawn then I yawn, too; There is noth-ing I can do.

Repeat one octave higher.

When your o - pen mouth I view, I can't help it, mine is, too!

After you are comfortable with this piece, try playing it in **C Position.**

Teacher Duet: Student plays one octave higher.

Note Guide

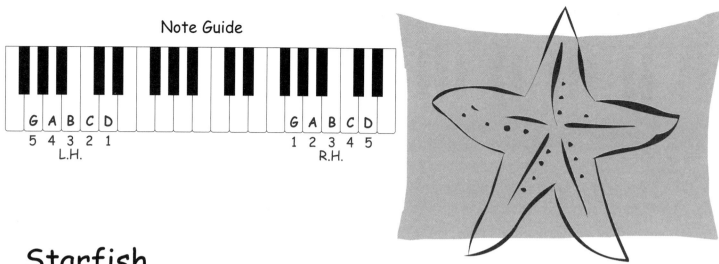

Starfish

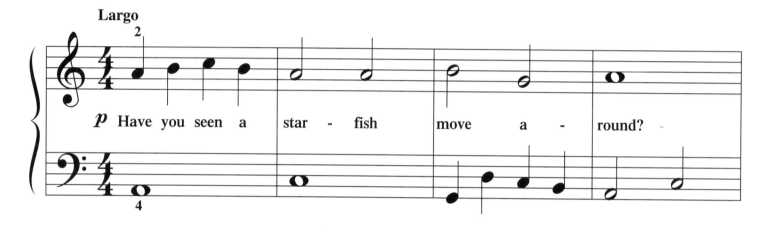

Largo

p Have you seen a star - fish move a - round?

5

Repeat one octave higher.

Do you think a star - fish makes a sound?

After you are comfortable with this piece, try playing with **R.H.** finger **3** on **A.**

Teacher Duet: Student plays one octave higher.

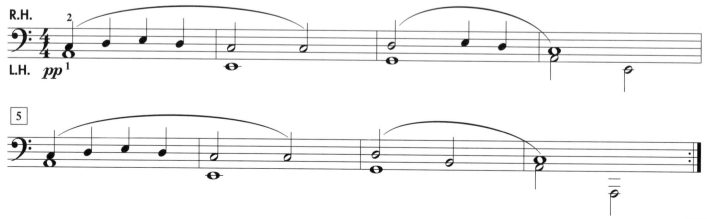

FJH2150

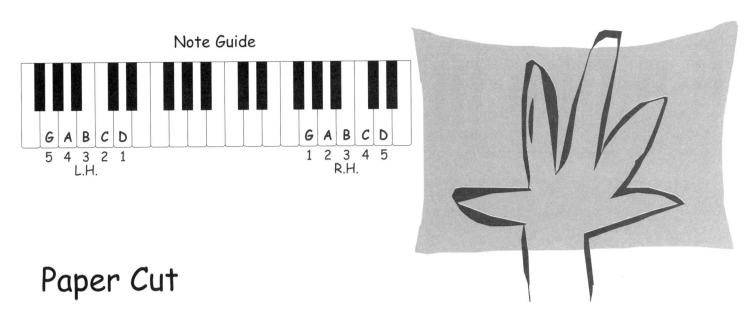

Paper Cut

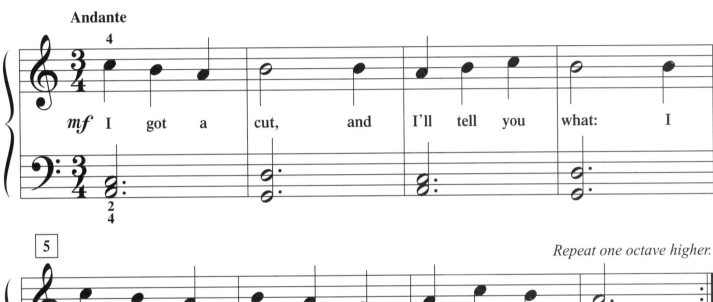

Andante

mf I got a cut, and I'll tell you what: I

Repeat one octave higher.

just did - n't know that a pa - per could cut.

After you are comfortable with this piece, try playing with **R.H.** finger **5** on **C.**

Teacher Duet: Student plays one octave higher.

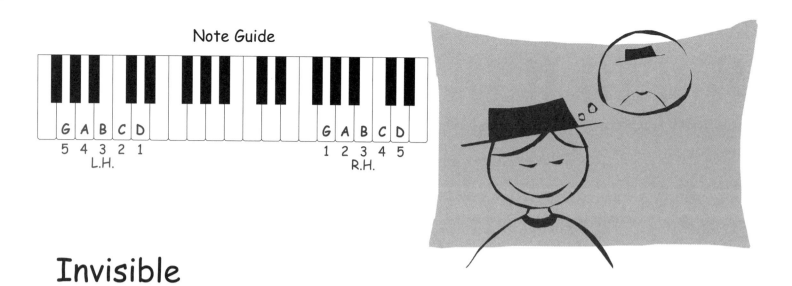

Invisible

Andante

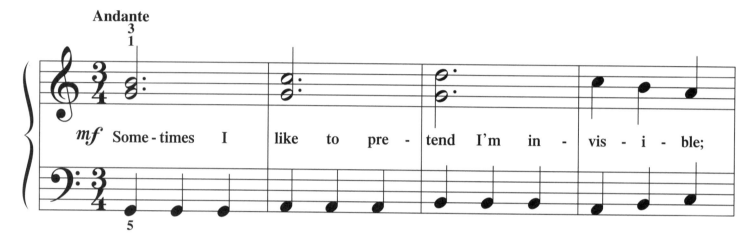

mf Some - times I like to pre - tend I'm in - vis - i - ble;

Repeat one octave higher.

No one can see me, it's so un - be - liev - a - ble!

After you are comfortable with this piece, try playing it in **C Position.**

Teacher Duet: Student plays one octave higher.

R.H.

L.H. *mp* *with pedal*

FJH2150

Treble G Hand Position*

The next group of notes in this book are in Treble G Position. To play in Treble G Position, place the left-hand thumb on the D above Middle C. Notice that the note sits in the space above the ledger line. Place the right-hand thumb on the G above Middle C. Place the rest of your fingers as indicated in the guide below.

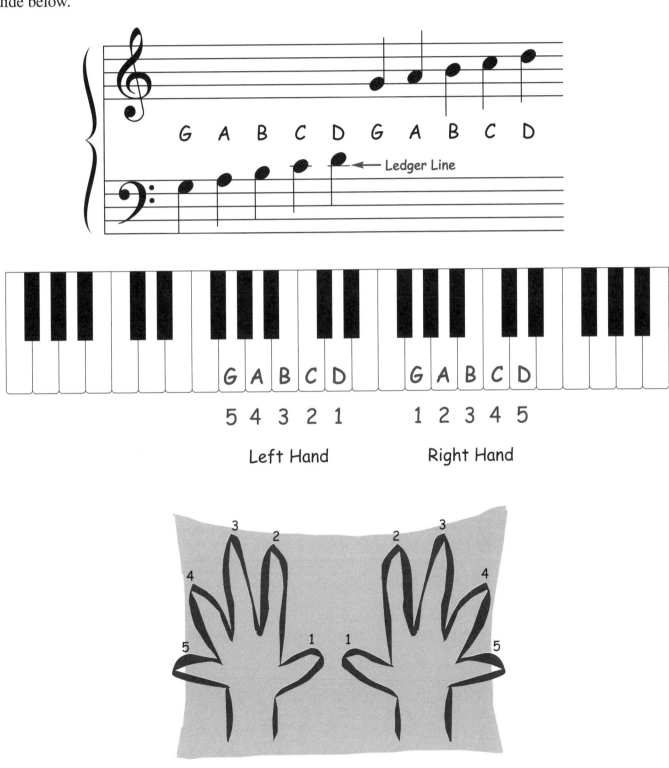

*Remember that hand positions are only "guides" that help you feel comfortable learning new notes. Once you are comfortable, remember to explore your pieces further by starting on a different finger.

G A B C D Higher on the Keyboard

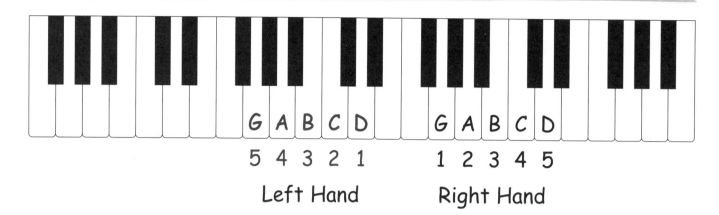

Remember that hand positions are just guides. When you are comfortable with the pieces in this unit, explore using different fingers.

G A B C D Higher on the Bass Staff

G Position

Play the example below, keeping your eyes on the music.

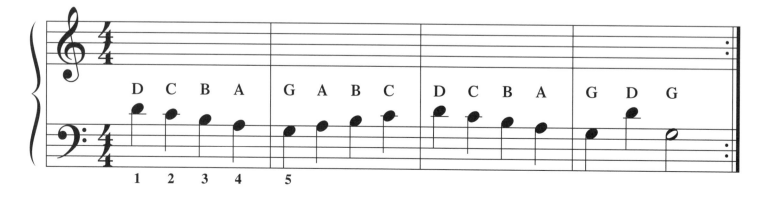

FJH2150

Note Guide

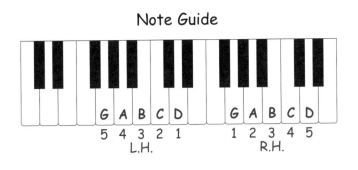

One Hundred Words

Allegro

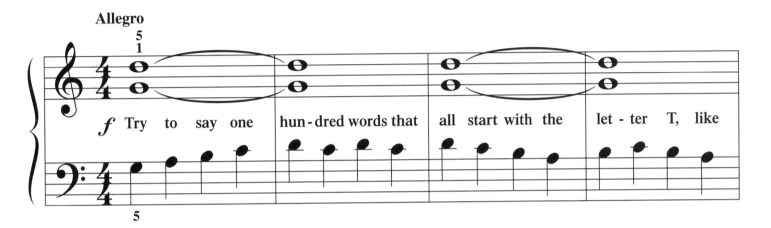

f Try to say one | hun-dred words that | all start with the | let-ter T, like

Repeat one octave higher.

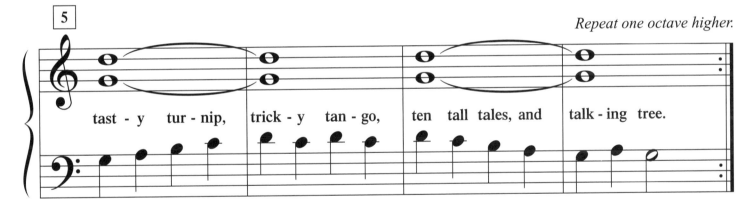

tast-y tur-nip, | trick-y tan-go, | ten tall tales, and | talk-ing tree.

After you are comfortable with this piece, try playing it in **C Position.**

Teacher Duet: Student plays one octave higher.

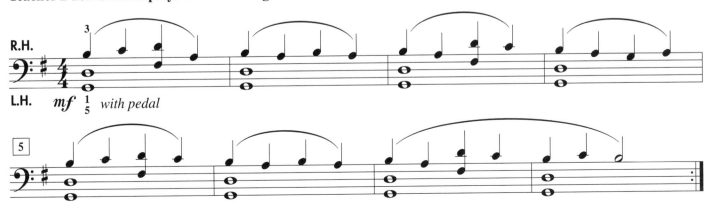

R.H.

L.H. *mf* *with pedal*

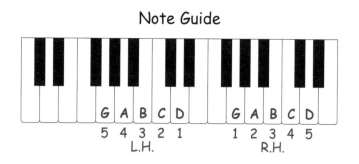

My Clean Room

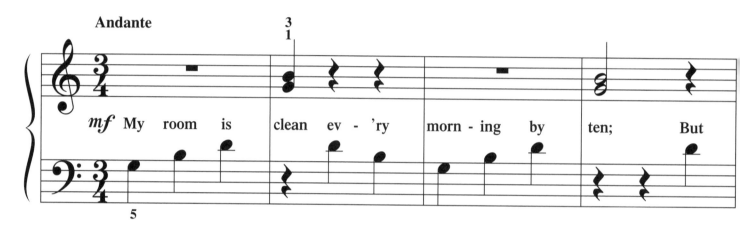

Andante

mf My room is clean ev - 'ry morn - ing by ten; But

Repeat one octave higher.

my broth - ers come and make mess - es a - gain.

After you are comfortable with this piece, try playing with **R.H.** fingers **2** and **4** on **G** and **B.**

Teacher Duet: Student plays one octave higher.

R.H.

L.H. *mp* *with pedal*

FJH2150

Note Guide

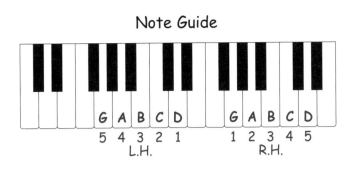

Jellyfish

I real - ly wish I had a jel - ly - fish. Oh,

Repeat one octave higher.

day af - ter day I'd love to watch it play.

After you are comfortable with this piece, try playing with **R.H.** fingers **2** and **4** on **G** and **B.**

Teacher Duet: Student plays one octave higher.

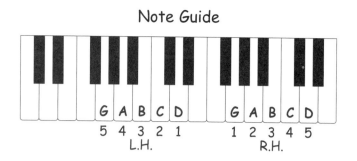

Note Guide

Cherries

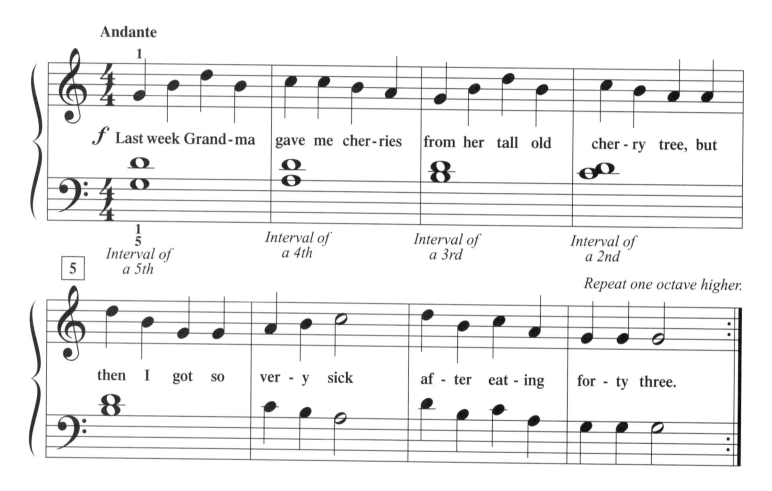

Andante

f Last week Grand-ma | gave me cher-ries | from her tall old | cher-ry tree, but

Interval of a 5th | *Interval of a 4th* | *Interval of a 3rd* | *Interval of a 2nd*

Repeat one octave higher.

then I got so | ver-y sick | af-ter eat-ing | for-ty three.

After you are comfortable with this piece, try playing it in another position.

Teacher Duet: Student plays as written.

mf

FJH2150

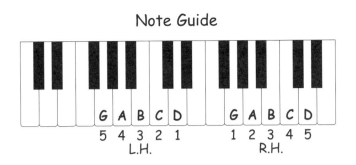

Note Guide

Fortune Cookies

Largo

mf For - tune cook - ies tell you things that are to come; My

5

Repeat one octave higher.

for - tune says that I will find some bub - ble gum.

After you are comfortable with this piece, try playing it in another position.

Teacher Duet: Student plays one octave higher.

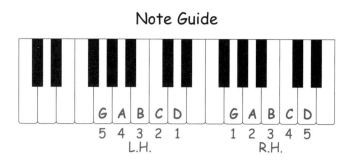

Toothpaste

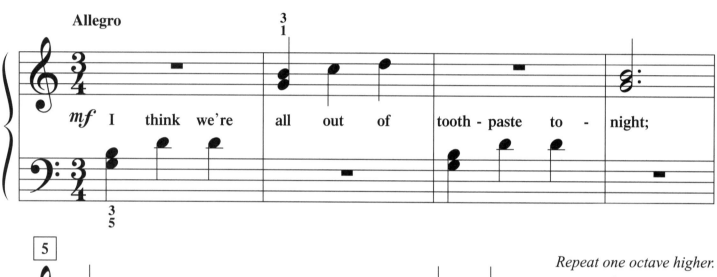

Allegro

mf I think we're all out of tooth - paste to - night;

Repeat one octave higher.

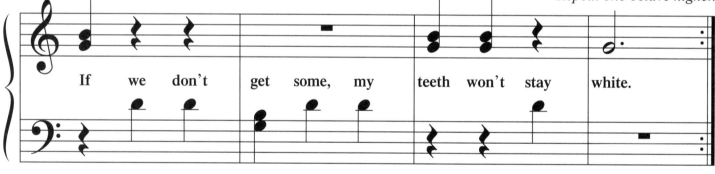

If we don't get some, my teeth won't stay white.

After you are comfortable with this piece, try playing it in another position.

Teacher Duet: Student plays one octave higher.

FJH2150

Note Guide

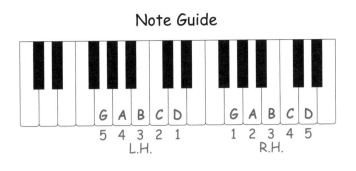

Leftovers

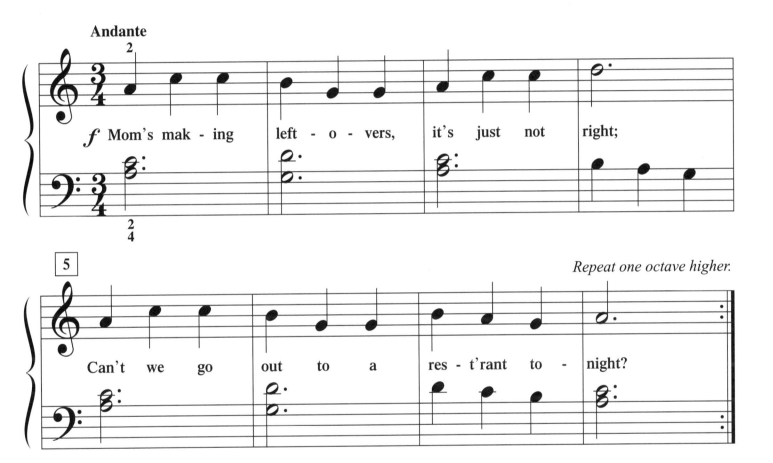

Andante

Mom's mak - ing left - o - vers, it's just not right;

Repeat one octave higher.

Can't we go out to a res - t'rant to - night?

After you are comfortable with this piece, try playing it in another position.

Teacher Duet: Student plays as written.

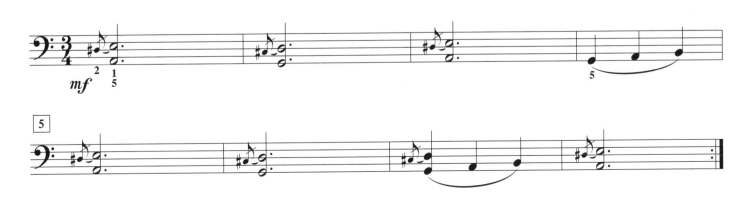

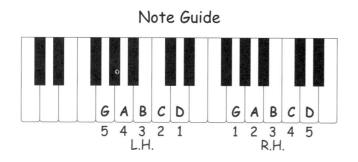

Note Guide

Watching Baseball

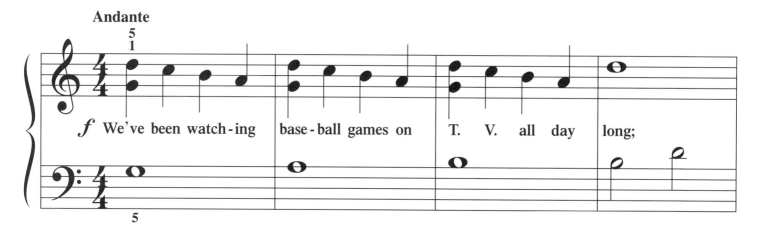

Andante

f We've been watch-ing base-ball games on T. V. all day long;

Repeat one octave higher.

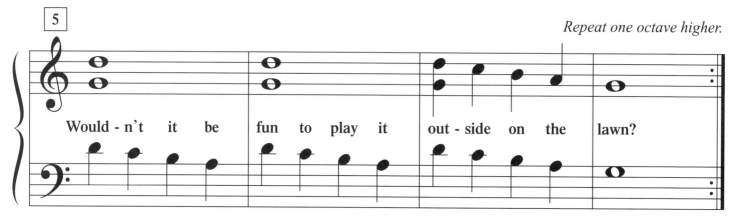

Would-n't it be fun to play it out-side on the lawn?

After you are comfortable with this piece, try playing it in another position.

Teacher Duet: Student plays one octave higher.

R.H.

L.H. *mf*

detached

44

FJH2150

F Hand Position*

The next group of notes in this book are in F Position. To play in F Position, place the left-hand thumb on Middle C and finger number 2 on the BLACK KEY just to the LEFT of B. This note is called B flat. Place the right-hand thumb on the F above Middle C and finger number 4 on the higher B flat. Place the rest of your fingers as indicated in the guide below.

*Remember that hand positions are only "guides" that help you feel comfortable learning new notes. Once you are comfortable, remember to explore your pieces further by starting on a different finger.

Unit 5   F G A B♭ C on the Keyboard

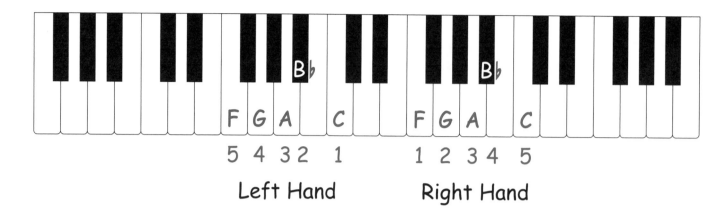

Left Hand   Right Hand

Remember that hand positions are just guides. When you are comfortable
with the pieces in this unit, explore using different fingers.

F G A B♭ C on the Treble and Bass Staff

F Position

F   G   A   B♭   C   F   G   A   B♭   C

Play the example below, keeping your eyes on the music.

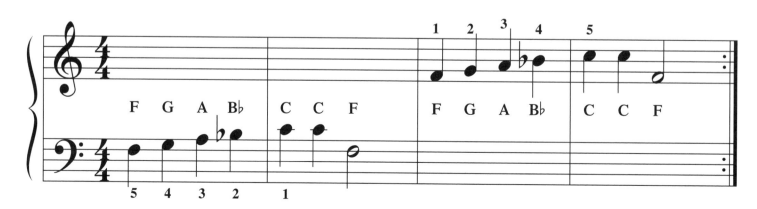

FJH2150

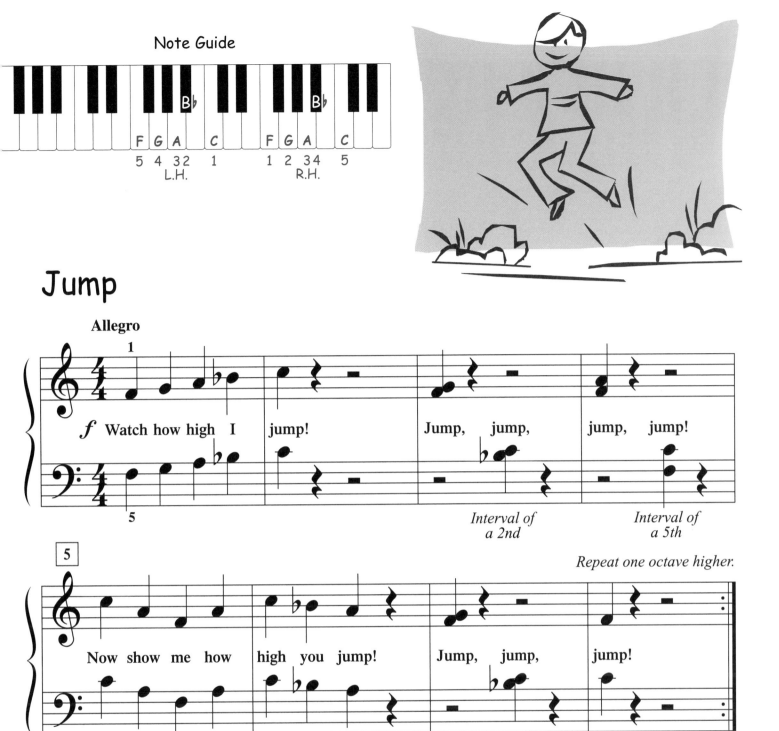

Jump

Allegro

f Watch how high I jump! Jump, jump, jump, jump!

Interval of a 2nd

Interval of a 5th

Repeat one octave higher.

Now show me how high you jump! Jump, jump, jump!

After you are comfortable with this piece, try playing it in another position.

Teacher Duet: Student plays as written.

R.H.

L.H. *mf*

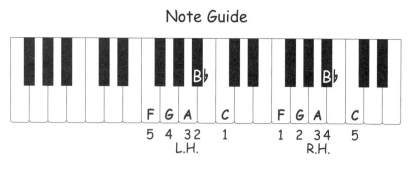

Note Guide

Hummingbird

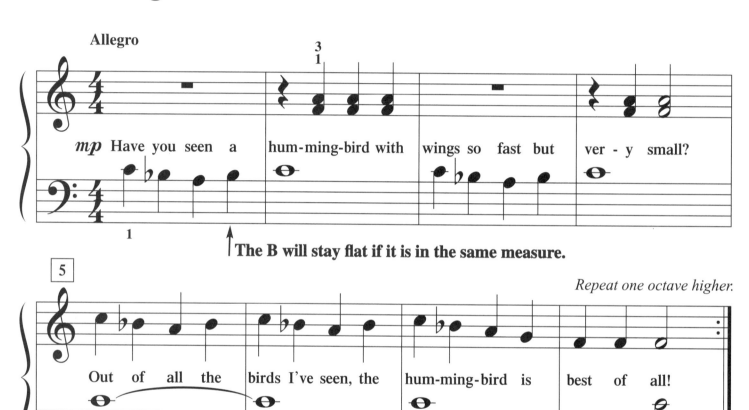

Allegro

mp Have you seen a hum-ming-bird with wings so fast but ver-y small?

↑ **The B will stay flat if it is in the same measure.**

Repeat one octave higher.

Out of all the birds I've seen, the hum-ming-bird is best of all!

After you are comfortable with this piece, try playing it in another position.

Teacher Duet: Student plays one octave higher.

FJH2150

Note Guide

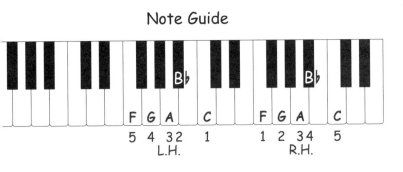

Tulip

Andante

mf Why do they call it a tu - lip?

5

Repeat one octave higher.

Why not a three or a four - lip?

After you are comfortable with this piece, try playing it in another position.

Teacher Duet: Student plays one octave higher.

R.H.

L.H. *mp* *with pedal*

5

Note Guide

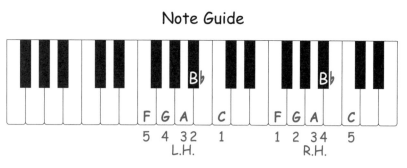

Travel Plans

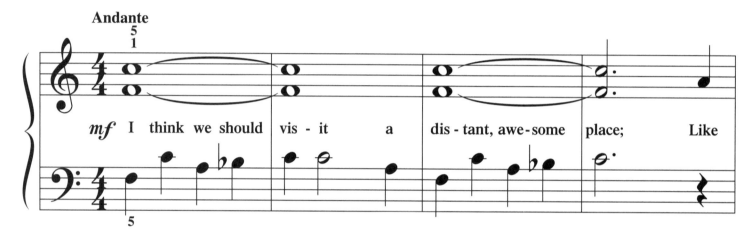

Andante

mf I think we should | vis - it a | dis - tant, awe-some | place; Like

Repeat one octave higher.

Chi - na or | Rus - sia or | e - ven out - er | space!

After you are comfortable with this piece, try playing it in another position.

Teacher Duet: Student plays one octave higher.

FJH2150

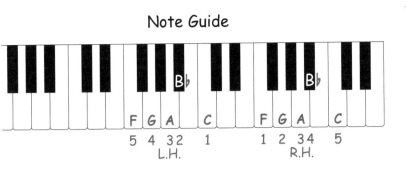

Checking the Mailbox

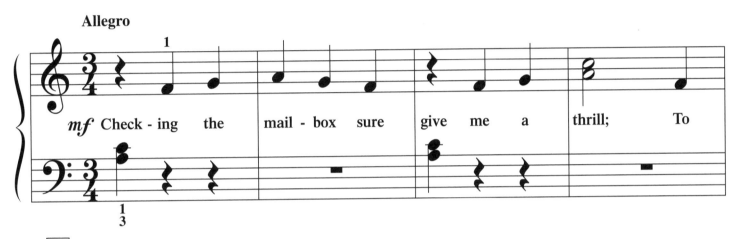

Allegro

mf Check - ing   the   mail - box   sure   give   me   a   thrill;   To

Repeat one octave higher.

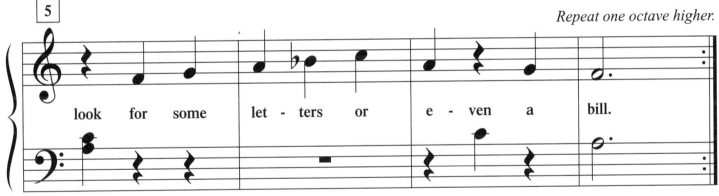

look   for   some   let - ters   or   e - ven   a   bill.

After you are comfortable with this piece, try playing with **L.H.** fingers **2** and **4** on **C** and **A.**

Teacher Duet: Student plays one octave higher.

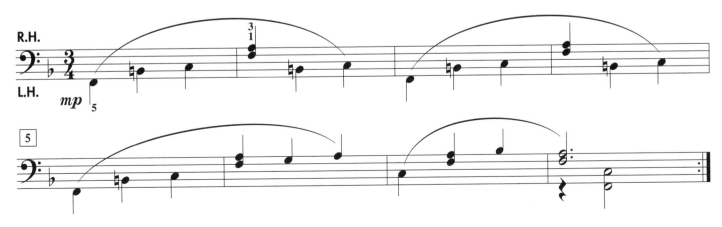

R.H.

L.H.   *mp*

Note Guide

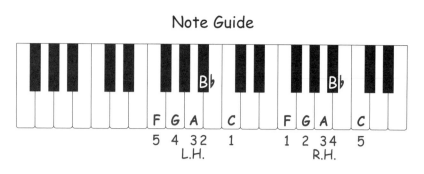

Slippers

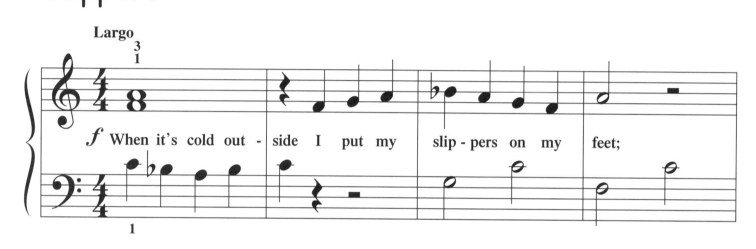

Largo

f When it's cold out - side I put my slip - pers on my feet;

5

Repeat one octave higher.

Slip - pers, my slip - pers, my slip - pers are so sweet!

After you are comfortable with this piece, try playing it in another position.

Teacher Duet: Student plays one octave higher.

mf

5

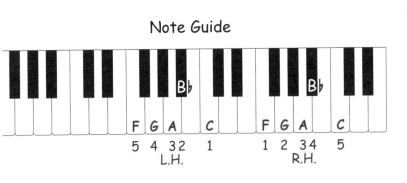

Note Guide

Walking My Frogs

Andante

mf All of my friends are out walk - ing their dogs. (ruff ruff)

Repeat one octave higher.

5

What will they think when I'm walk - ing my frogs? (rib - bit)

After you are comfortable with this piece, try playing it in another position.

Teacher Duet: Student plays one octave higher.

R.H.

L.H. mp

5

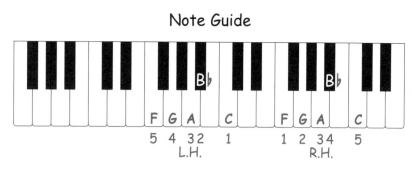

Lazy

Largo

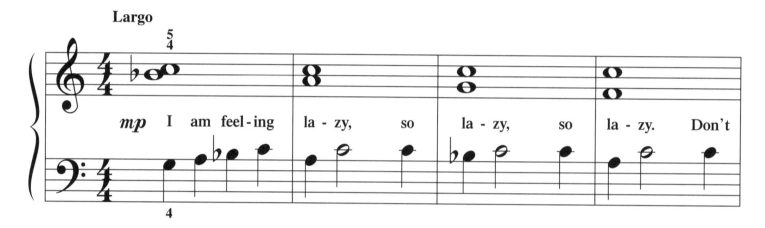

mp I am feel-ing la - zy, so la - zy, so la - zy. Don't

Repeat one octave higher.

bug me when I'm la - zy; I just don't want to work.

After you are comfortable with this piece, try playing it in another position.

Teacher Duet: Student plays one octave higher.

54

D Hand Position*

The next group of notes in this book are in D Position. To play in D Position, place the left-hand thumb on the A below Middle C and finger number 3 on the BLACK KEY just to the RIGHT of F. This note is called F sharp. Place the right-hand thumb on the D above Middle C and finger number 3 on the higher F sharp. Place the rest of your fingers as indicated in the guide below.

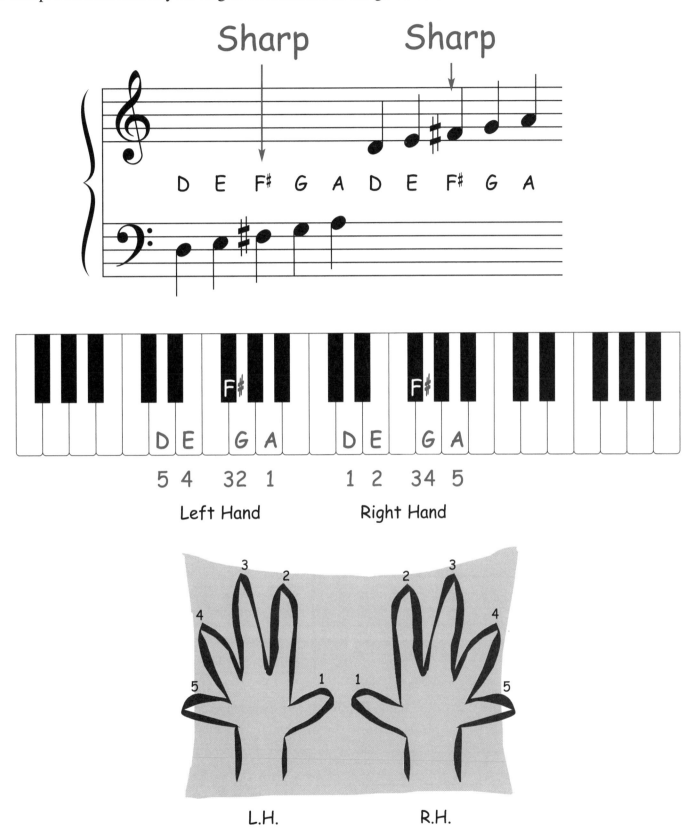

*Remember that hand positions are only "guides" that help you feel comfortable learning new notes. Once you are comfortable, remember to explore your pieces further by starting on a different finger.

Unit 6 — D E F# G A on the Keyboard

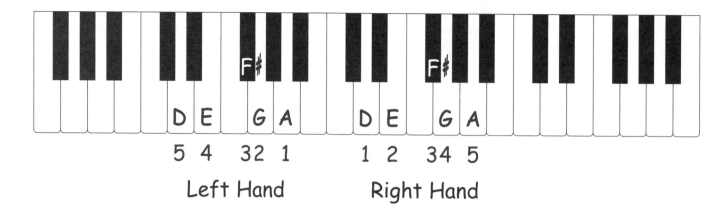

Remember that hand positions are just guides. When you are comfortable with the pieces in this unit, explore using different fingers.

D E F# G A on the Treble and Bass Staff

D Position

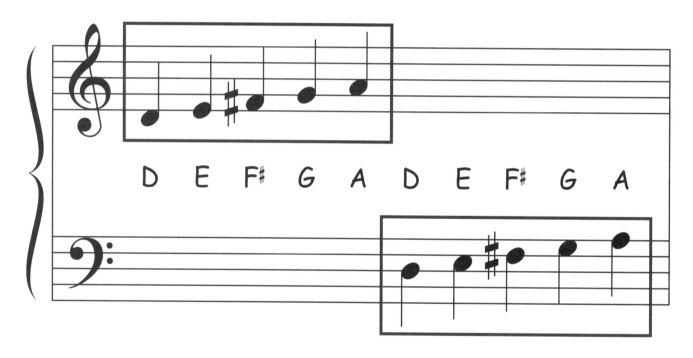

Play the example below, keeping your eyes on the music.

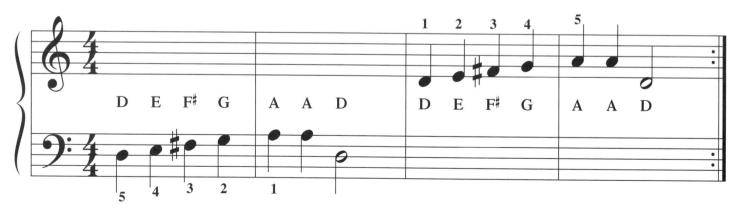

FJH2150

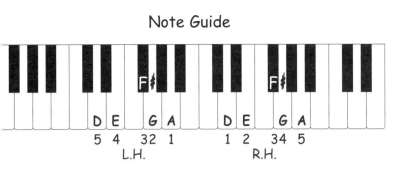

Note Guide

Rules for April Fools

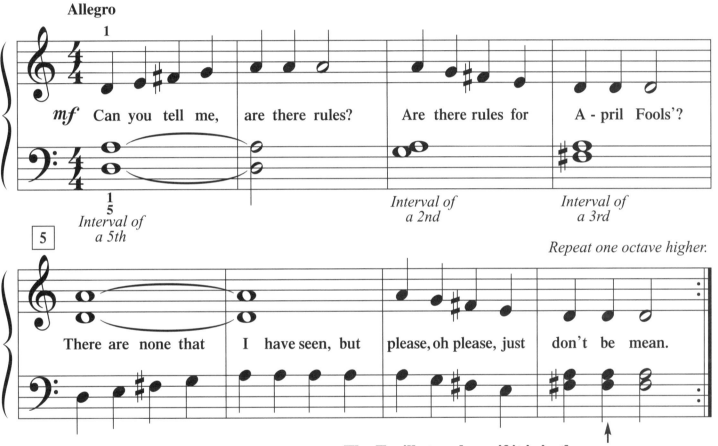

Allegro

mf Can you tell me, are there rules? Are there rules for A - pril Fools'?

Interval of a 5th

Interval of a 2nd

Interval of a 3rd

Repeat one octave higher.

There are none that I have seen, but please, oh please, just don't be mean.

The F will stay sharp if it is in the same measure.

After you are comfortable with this piece, try playing it in another position.

Teacher Duet: Student plays one octave higher.

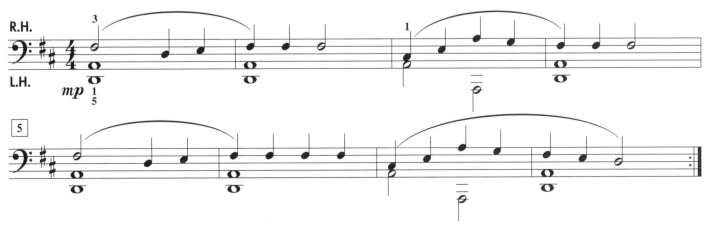

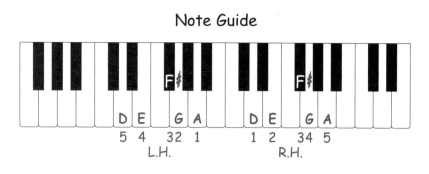

Note Guide

My Umbrella

Andante

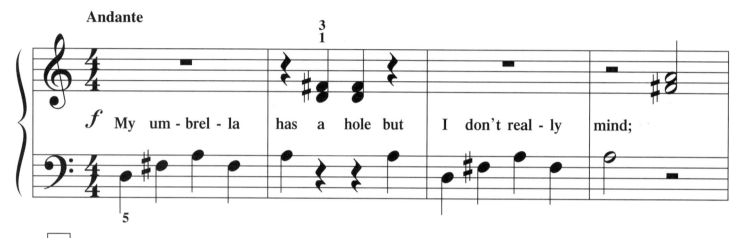

f My um-brel-la   has a hole but   I don't real-ly   mind;

Repeat one octave higher.

If it rains, then   I will feel just   one drop at a   time.

After you are comfortable with this piece, try playing it in another position.

Teacher Duet: Student plays one octave higher.

FJH2150

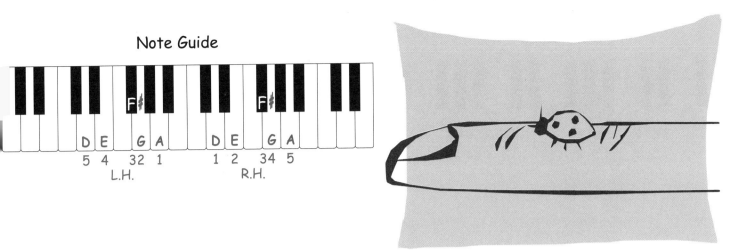

Note Guide

Ladybug

Largo

mp La - dy - bug, la - dy - bug, don't fly a - way.

Repeat one octave higher.

Please, won't you stay on my fin - ger all day?

After you are comfortable with this piece, try playing it in another position.

Teacher Duet: Student plays one octave higher.

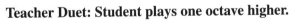

R.H.

L.H. *p* *with pedal*

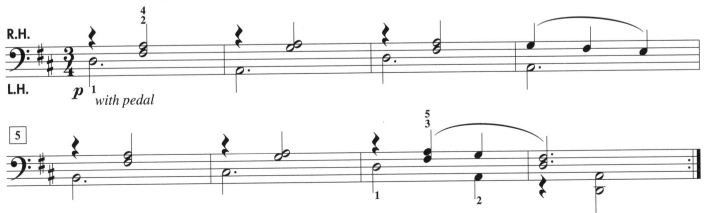

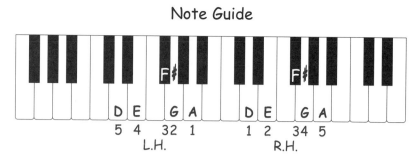

Note Guide

Smoothie

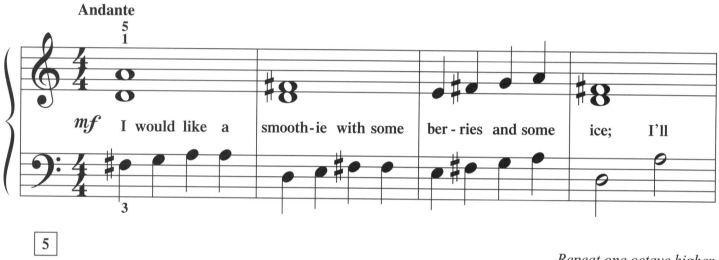

Andante

mf I would like a | smooth-ie with some | ber - ries and some | ice; I'll

Repeat one octave higher.

blend it up and | take a drink, I'm | sure it will taste | nice.

After you are comfortable with this piece, try playing it in another position.

Teacher Duet: Student plays one octave higher.

R.H.

L.H.

mp

60

FJH2150

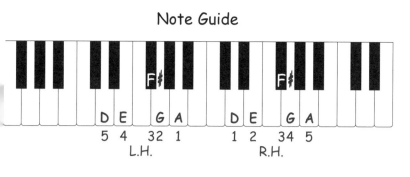

Note Guide

Icicles

Andante

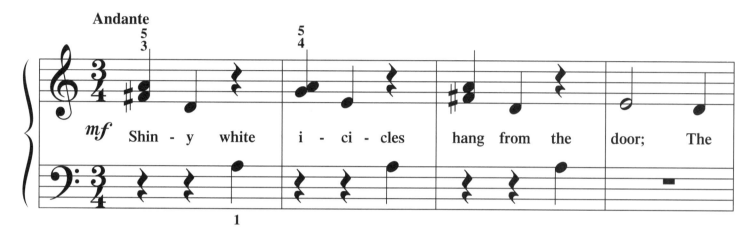

Shin - y   white   i - ci - cles   hang from the   door;   The

Repeat one octave higher.

5

next   time   it's   snow - ing   then   we'll   get   some   more.

After you are comfortable with this piece, try playing with **L.H.** finger **2** on **A.**

Teacher Duet: Student plays one octave higher.

Note Guide

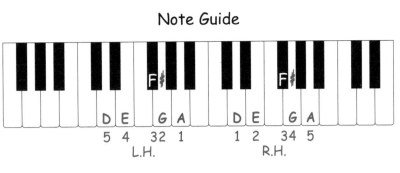

Socks Shocks

Allegro

f Some-times when I'm | wear-ing socks | on the car-pet, | I get shocks.

5

Repeat one octave higher.

Do you know why | this could be? | Stat - ic e - lec - tric - i - ty!

After you are comfortable with this piece, try playing it in another position.

Teacher Duet: Student plays one octave higher.

mf

detached

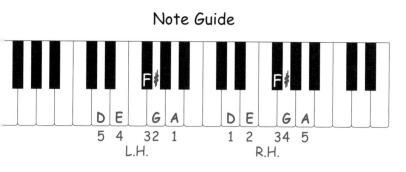

Note Guide

Broken Watch

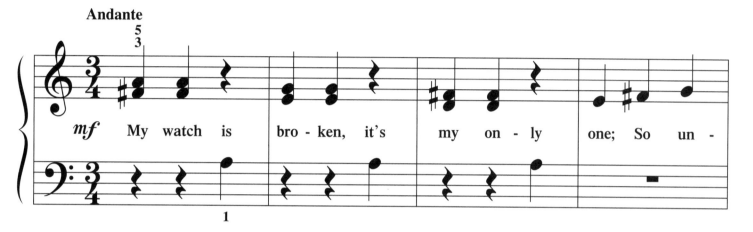

Andante

mf My watch is | bro - ken, it's | my on - ly | one; So un -

Repeat one octave higher.

til it is | fixed, I'll tell | time by the | sun.

After you are comfortable with this piece, try playing it in another position.

Teacher Duet: Student plays as written.

JH2150

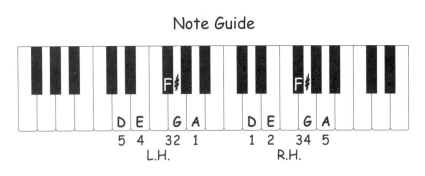

Note Guide

End of the Book

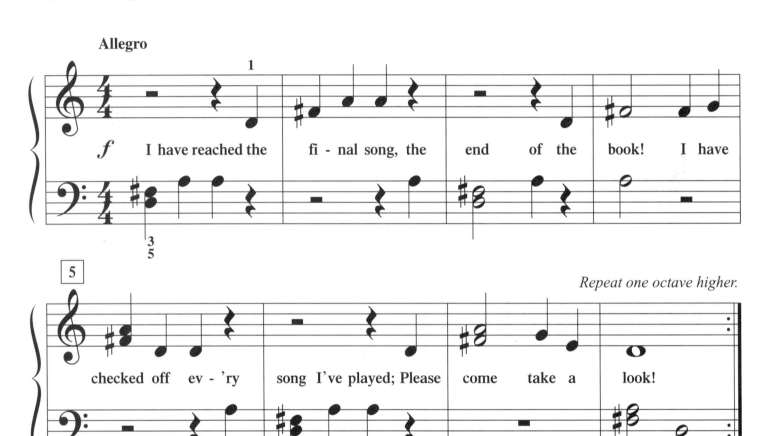

Allegro

f I have reached the | fi - nal song, the | end of the | book! I have

5

checked off ev - 'ry | song I've played; Please | come take a | look!

Repeat one octave higher.

After you are comfortable with this piece, try playing it in another position.

Teacher Duet: Student plays one octave higher.

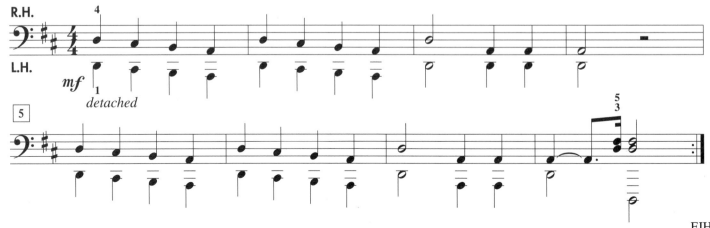